First World War
and Army of Occupation
War Diary
France, Belgium and Germany

16 DIVISION
Divisional Troops
'C' Squadron South Irish Horse
19 December 1915 - 31 May 1916

WO95/1962/1

The Naval & Military Press Ltd
www.nmarchive.com
Published in association with The National Archives

Published by

The Naval & Military Press Ltd

Unit 10 Ridgewood Industrial Park,

Uckfield, East Sussex,

TN22 5QE England

Tel: +44 (0) 1825 749494

www.naval-military-press.com

www.nmarchive.com

This diary has been reprinted in facsimile from the original. Any imperfections are inevitably reproduced and the quality may fall short of modern type and cartographic standards.

© **Crown Copyright**
Images reproduced by permission of The National Archives, London, England, 2015.

Contents

Document type	Place/Title	Date From	Date To
Heading	WO95/1962 (II)		
Heading	16th Division "C" Sqdn 8th Irish Horse. Dec 1915-May 1916		
Heading	War Diary Of C. Sqdn South Irish Horse (16th Divisional Cavalry) From 19th Dec 1915 To 31.12.15		
War Diary	Havre	19/12/1915	19/12/1915
War Diary	Fouquereuil	20/12/1915	20/12/1915
War Diary	Labuis-Siere	21/12/1915	24/12/1915
War Diary	France	24/12/1915	24/12/1915
War Diary	Labuis-Siere	25/12/1915	26/12/1915
War Diary	Labuis-Siere France	27/12/1915	28/12/1915
War Diary	Westrehem.	29/12/1915	31/12/1915
Heading	C Sq. S. Irish Horse Vol. I Jan 16		
War Diary	Westrehem	01/01/1916	31/01/1916
Heading	War Diary "C" Sqdn South Irish House May 1916 Vol 5		
Heading	C Sqdn South Irish Horse War Diary-February 1916 Vol 2		
War Diary	Westrehem	01/02/1916	27/02/1916
War Diary	Cantrainne	28/02/1916	29/02/1916
Heading	C Sqdn South Irish Horse War Diary-March 1916 Vol 3		
War Diary	Cantrainne	01/03/1916	08/03/1916
War Diary	HurionVille	09/03/1916	27/03/1916
War Diary	Vaudricourt	28/03/1916	31/03/1916
Heading	War Diary "C" Squadron-South Irish Horse Month Of April 1916 Vol 4		
War Diary	Vaudricourt	01/04/1916	31/05/1916

w995 / 1962(11) / 1963(20)

16TH DIVISION

'C' SQDN 5TH IRISH HORSE.

DEC 1915 - MAY 1916

Confidential

War Diary

of

C. Sqdn South Irish Horse
(16th Divisional Cavalry)

From 19th Dec 1915 to ~~31.12.15~~ to ~~31st Jan 1916~~

Army Form C. 2118

WAR DIARY
or
INTELLIGENCE SUMMARY
(Erase heading not required.)

Instructions regarding War Diaries and Intelligence Summaries are contained in F. S. Regs., Part II. and the Staff Manual respectively. Title Pages will be prepared in manuscript.

Place	Date	Hour	Summary of Events and Information	Remarks and references to Appendices
HAVRE	19/12/15	7 a.m.	Arrived in France from SOUTHAMPTON, after moderate passage, which new and horses stood well. Two slight casualties amongst horses. Left by train for destination 7.45 p.m. Fine cold weather.	

A E Denny
Major

WAR DIARY
or
INTELLIGENCE SUMMARY

Army Form C. 2118

Place	Date	Hour	Summary of Events and Information	Remarks and references to Appendices
FOUQUER-EIL	20/12/15		Arrived FOUQUEREIL STATION where we	
		4.30 pm	detrained.	
		6 pm	Left by road for LABUISSIERE where we were to be billeted. Arrived 7.15 p.m. which was in bad condition on our arrival. Men in barns. Fine cold weather.	

A. E. Berry / Major

Army Form C. 2118

WAR DIARY
or
INTELLIGENCE SUMMARY
(Erase heading not required.)

Instructions regarding War Diaries and Intelligence Summaries are contained in F.S. Regs., Part II. and the Staff Manual respectively. Title Pages will be prepared in manuscript.

Place	Date	Hour	Summary of Events and Information	Remarks and references to Appendices
LABUIS-SIERE	21/12/15		Nothing unusual occurred today. Rainy weather.	

Moss Major
3/6

WAR DIARY or INTELLIGENCE SUMMARY

Army Form C. 2118

Place	Date	Hour	Summary of Events and Information	Remarks and references to Appendices
LABUIS-SIERE	22/12/15		Nothing unusual occurred today. Rainy weather.	

A.G. Snow Major
N.3.6.

Army Form C. 2118

WAR DIARY
or
INTELLIGENCE SUMMARY
(Erase heading not required.)

Place	Date	Hour	Summary of Events and Information	Remarks and references to Appendices
LABUIS-SIERE	23/12/15.		Nothing unusual occurred today. Rainy weather with cold wind.	

Army Form C. 2118

WAR DIARY
or
INTELLIGENCE SUMMARY

(Erase heading not required.)

Instructions regarding War Diaries and Intelligence Summaries are contained in F. S. Regs., Part II. and the Staff Manual respectively. Title Pages will be prepared in manuscript.

Place	Date	Hour	Summary of Events and Information	Remarks and references to Appendices
LABUIS-SIERE- FRANCE	24/12/15		Nothing unusual occurred today. Fine day, but cold.	

H E Brown Major.

WAR DIARY or INTELLIGENCE SUMMARY

(Erase heading not required.)

Army Form C. 2118

Place	Date	Hour	Summary of Events and Information	Remarks and references to Appendices
LABUIS-SIERE	25/12/15		Christmas Day. Nothing unusual occurred today. Showery day.	

Place	Date	Hour	Summary of Events and Information	Remarks and references to Appendices
LABUIS-SIERE	26/12/15		Nothing unusual occurred today. Horse lines which were in a very bad state after all the rain were moved to another field adjoining. G.O.C 16th Division inspected the Camp and decided to move the unit, as horses were losing condition in their present state in the open, and absolutely no huts were had, there being no horse billets available where the men could mess. Fine day. N S Cowly Major	

Army Form C. 2118

WAR DIARY
or
INTELLIGENCE SUMMARY

(Erase heading not required.)

Instructions regarding War Diaries and Intelligence Summaries are contained in F. S. Regs., Part II. and the Staff Manual respectively. Title Pages will be prepared in manuscript.

Place	Date	Hour	Summary of Events and Information	Remarks and references to Appendices
LABUIS-SIERE	2/10/15		Nothing unusual occurred today. Fine weather.	
FRANCE				

H E Bonny Major.

WAR DIARY
INTELLIGENCE SUMMARY

Army Form C. 2118

Place	Date	Hour	Summary of Events and Information	Remarks and references to Appendices
LABUIS-SIERE FRANCE	28/12/15		I have had to be destroyed, his leg being broken by a kick.	

H.E.Bovey
Major

WAR DIARY
or
INTELLIGENCE SUMMARY

(Erase heading not required.)

Army Form C. 2118

Place	Date	Hour	Summary of Events and Information	Remarks and references to Appendices
WESTRE-HEM.	29/10/15		Left LABUISSIERE 9 am by road and arrived WESTREHEM 2.30 pm. Advance Party preceded main body & secured billets for Officers, men, & accommodation for horses. No casualties to men or horses on the journey. Fine day. Roads along the route in good condition.	

A. E. Beatty Major

Place	Date	Hour	Summary of Events and Information	Remarks and references to Appendices
WESTRE-HEM	30/12/15		Nothing unusual occurred today. Fine day.	

F.E. Bave Major

WAR DIARY
or
INTELLIGENCE SUMMARY

(Erase heading not required.)

Army Form C. 2118

Place	Date	Hour	Summary of Events and Information	Remarks and references to Appendices
WESTRE HEM	31/12/15		Nothing unusual occurred today. Showery weather.	

F E Brown Major

16

Army Form C. 2118

WAR DIARY
or
INTELLIGENCE SUMMARY

(Erase heading not required.)

Instructions regarding War Diaries and Intelligence Summaries are contained in F. S. Regs., Part II. and the Staff Manual respectively. Title Pages will be prepared in manuscript.

Place	Date	Hour	Summary of Events and Information	Remarks and references to Appendices
WESTRE-HEM.	1/1/16		Nothing unusual occurred today. Raining day.	

H.E. Grey Major

Army Form C. 2118

WAR DIARY
or
INTELLIGENCE SUMMARY
(Erase heading not required.)

Place	Date	Hour	Summary of Events and Information	Remarks and references to Appendices
WESTRE-HEM	2/1/16		Major H. Bury & Capt Trant attended a Conference at Divisional Head Qrs at Bomy. Wet day.	

F.E. Brown / Major

Place	Date	Hour	Summary of Events and Information	Remarks and references to Appendices
WESTRE-HEM	3/1/16		Nothing unusual occurred today. 2/Lt Cathcart left for Divisional HQrs to take up post of Composition Officer. Fine day.	

A.E. Donny / Major

Place	Date	Hour	Summary of Events and Information	Remarks and references to Appendices
WESTRE-HEM.	4/1/16		Nothing unusual occurred today. Raining day.	

F.E. Berry Major

WAR DIARY
or
INTELLIGENCE SUMMARY

Army Form C. 2118

Place	Date	Hour	Summary of Events and Information	Remarks and references to Appendices
WESTRE-HEM.	5/1/16.		44 men from the Squadron employed on Police Duty, in connection with Scheme, being carried out by the 15th Division. 4 a.m. 1st Squadron left WESTREHEM placed on the route. Fine sunny day.	

J E Moore
Major

WAR DIARY
or
INTELLIGENCE SUMMARY

(Erase heading not required.)

Army Form C. 2118

Place	Date	Hour	Summary of Events and Information	Remarks and references to Appendices
WESTRE-HEM	6/1/16		Nothing unusual occurred today. Wet day	

A. E. Brown Major

Place	Date	Hour	Summary of Events and Information	Remarks and references to Appendices
WESTRE-HEM	7/1/16		24 men employed on Pasha Dug in connexion with Scheme being carried out by 15th Division. Left WESTREHEM 4.30 am for VAUCOURT points en route. Showery day.	

Lt E Perry Major

Army Form C. 2118

WAR DIARY
or
INTELLIGENCE SUMMARY
(Erase heading not required.)

Instructions regarding War Diaries and Intelligence Summaries are contained in F. S. Regs., Part II. and the Staff Manual respectively. Title Pages will be prepared in manuscript.

Place	Date	Hour	Summary of Events and Information	Remarks and references to Appendices
WESTRE-HEM	8/1/16		Nothing unusual occurred today	

Lares O.3.16

Army Form C. 2118

WAR DIARY
or
INTELLIGENCE SUMMARY
(Erase heading not required.)

Place	Date	Hour	Summary of Events and Information	Remarks and references to Appendices
MESTRE-HEM	9/1/16		"Nothing unusual occurred today. Fine day	

Major

WAR DIARY
or
INTELLIGENCE SUMMARY

(Erase heading not required.)

Army Form C. 2118

Place	Date	Hour	Summary of Events and Information	Remarks and references to Appendices
WESTRE-AEM.	16/1/16		Nothing unusual occurred today. Showery weather.	

J. E. Barry
Major

Place	Date	Hour	Summary of Events and Information	Remarks and references to Appendices
WESTRE-HEM	11/1/16		Nothing unusual occurred today	

F.E. Cooper Major

Place	Date	Hour	Summary of Events and Information	Remarks and references to Appendices
WESTRE-HEM	12/1/16		Nothing unusual occurred today	

H.E. Berry Major

WAR DIARY or INTELLIGENCE SUMMARY

Army Form C. 2118

Place	Date	Hour	Summary of Events and Information	Remarks and references to Appendices
NESTRE-AEN.	13/1/16		Nothing unusual occurred today	

F. E. Berry / Major

Army Form C. 2118

WAR DIARY
or
INTELLIGENCE SUMMARY
(Erase heading not required.)

Instructions regarding War Diaries and Intelligence Summaries are contained in F. S. Regs., Part II. and the Staff Manual respectively. Title Pages will be prepared in manuscript.

Place	Date	Hour	Summary of Events and Information	Remarks and references to Appendices
WESTRE-HEM	14/11/16		Nothing unusual occurred today	

J. E. Berry
Major

WAR DIARY or INTELLIGENCE SUMMARY

Army Form C. 2118

Place	Date	Hour	Summary of Events and Information	Remarks and references to Appendices
WESTRE-HEM	15/1/16		Nothing unusual occurred today.	

J.E. Berry / Major

WAR DIARY
INTELLIGENCE SUMMARY

Place	Date	Hour	Summary of Events and Information	Remarks and references to Appendices
WESTRE-HEM	16/1/16		Nothing unusual occurred today	

J. E. Berry / Major

Army Form C. 2118

WAR DIARY
or
INTELLIGENCE SUMMARY
(Erase heading not required.)

Place	Date	Hour	Summary of Events and Information	Remarks and references to Appendices
WESTRE-HEM	17/1/16		Nothing unusual occurred today	

A. E. Berry / Major

WAR DIARY
or
INTELLIGENCE SUMMARY

(Erase heading not required.)

Army Form C. 2118

Place	Date	Hour	Summary of Events and Information	Remarks and references to Appendices
WESTRE-HEM	18/1/16		Nothing unusual occurred today	

A. E. Derry / Major

Army Form C. 2118

WAR DIARY
~~INTELLIGENCE SUMMARY~~
(Erase heading not required.)

Instructions regarding War Diaries and Intelligence Summaries are contained in F. S. Regs., Part II. and the Staff Manual respectively. Title Pages will be prepared in manuscript.

Place	Date	Hour	Summary of Events and Information	Remarks and references to Appendices
WESTRE-HEM	9/11/15		Nothing unusual occurred today.	

F.E.Berry /Major

WAR DIARY or INTELLIGENCE SUMMARY

Army Form C. 2118

Place	Date	Hour	Summary of Events and Information	Remarks and references to Appendices
WESTRE-HEM	20/1/16		60 men from Squadron occupied in policing route traversed by Gen Joffre showing day.	

A.E. Brown / Major

WAR DIARY
or
INTELLIGENCE SUMMARY

(Erase heading not required.)

Army Form C. 2118

Place	Date	Hour	Summary of Events and Information	Remarks and references to Appendices
WESTRE-HEM.	2/1/16		Nothing unusual occurred today.	

J.E.Goody / Major

WAR DIARY or INTELLIGENCE SUMMARY

Army Form C. 2118

Place	Date	Hour	Summary of Events and Information	Remarks and references to Appendices
WESTRE-HEM.	22/1/16		Nothing of unusual occurred today	

A.E. Brown
Major

WAR DIARY
INTELLIGENCE SUMMARY

Army Form C. 2118

Place	Date	Hour	Summary of Events and Information	Remarks and references to Appendices
WESTRE-HEM	23/1/16		Nothing unusual occurred today.	

J.E.Berry Major

Place	Date	Hour	Summary of Events and Information	Remarks and references to Appendices
WESTRE- HEM.	24/11/16		Nothing unusual occurred today. Showery weather	

J.E.Boorn Major

WAR DIARY
or
INTELLIGENCE SUMMARY

(Erase heading not required.)

Army Form C. 2118

Place	Date	Hour	Summary of Events and Information	Remarks and references to Appendices
MESNRE-HEM.	23/11/16		Nothing unusual occurred to-day. Fine day.	

H.E.G. Curry / Major

WAR DIARY
or
INTELLIGENCE SUMMARY

Army Form C. 2118

Place	Date	Hour	Summary of Events and Information	Remarks and references to Appendices
WESTRE HEM.	26/1/16		All horses of the Squadron were inoculated by new French process. Fine weather.	

J E Berry / Major

WAR DIARY
or
INTELLIGENCE SUMMARY

(Erase heading not required.)

Army Form C. 2118

Instructions regarding War Diaries and Intelligence Summaries are contained in F. S. Regs., Part II. and the Staff Manual respectively. Title Pages will be prepared in manuscript.

Place	Date	Hour	Summary of Events and Information	Remarks and references to Appendices
WESTREHEM.	27/11/16		Nothing unusual occurred today. Fine weather.	

H E Doney / Major

WAR DIARY
or
INTELLIGENCE SUMMARY

(Erase heading not required.)

Army Form C. 2118

Instructions regarding War Diaries and Intelligence Summaries are contained in F. S. Regs., Part II. and the Staff Manual respectively. Title Pages will be prepared in manuscript.

Place	Date	Hour	Summary of Events and Information	Remarks and references to Appendices
WESTRE-HEM	28/1/16		Nothing unusual occurred today. Fine weather	

A. E. Down / Major

Army Form C. 2118

WAR DIARY
or
INTELLIGENCE SUMMARY
(Erase heading not required.)

Instructions regarding War Diaries and Intelligence Summaries are contained in F.S. Regs., Part II. and the Staff Manual respectively. Title Pages will be prepared in manuscript.

Place	Date	Hour	Summary of Events and Information	Remarks and references to Appendices
WESTRE HEM.	29/1/16		Nothing unusual occurred today. Fine weather.	

A.E.Brown Major

WAR DIARY
or
INTELLIGENCE SUMMARY

Army Form C. 2118

Place	Date	Hour	Summary of Events and Information	Remarks and references to Appendices
NESTRE-HEM	30/1/16		2/Lts HOGARTY and BRODIE left to attend young officers school at LILLERS. Good weather.	

Maro C6 2/6 Major

Place	Date	Hour	Summary of Events and Information	Remarks and references to Appendices
WESTRE HEM	31/1/16		Nothing unusual occurred today. Fine day.	

A.E. Bony Major

C.S.I. Horse
Vol 5

Confidential

War Diary

"C Sqd" South Irish Horse

May 1916

16

"C" Sqdn - South Irish Horse Vol 2

Confidential

C. Sqdn - South Irish Horse.

War Diary - February 1916

WAR DIARY
or
INTELLIGENCE SUMMARY

Army Form C. 2118

Place	Date	Hour	Summary of Events and Information	Remarks and references to Appendices
WESTRE HEM	1/2/16		Nothing unusual occurred today.	

A.E Berry Major

WAR DIARY
or
INTELLIGENCE SUMMARY

(Erase heading not required.)

Army Form C. 2118

Place	Date	Hour	Summary of Events and Information	Remarks and references to Appendices
MESIRE HEM.	2/9/16		Nothing unusual occurred today	

A.E.Berry Major

Army Form C. 2118

WAR DIARY
or
INTELLIGENCE SUMMARY

(Erase heading not required.)

Instructions regarding War Diaries and Intelligence Summaries are contained in F. S. Regs., Part II. and the Staff Manual respectively. Title Pages will be prepared in manuscript.

Place	Date	Hour	Summary of Events and Information	Remarks and references to Appendices
WESTRE AEM.	3/9/16		Nothing unusual occurred today	

J E Berry
Major

WAR DIARY
or
INTELLIGENCE SUMMARY

Army Form C. 2118

Place	Date	Hour	Summary of Events and Information	Remarks and references to Appendices
WESTRE HEM	4/3/16		Nothing unusual occurred today	

H E Berry Major

Army Form C. 2118

WAR DIARY
or
INTELLIGENCE SUMMARY
(Erase heading not required.)

Place	Date	Hour	Summary of Events and Information	Remarks and references to Appendices
WESTRE-HEN.	5/2/16		Nothing unusual occurred today.	

H E Beazley Major

WAR DIARY
or
INTELLIGENCE SUMMARY

(Erase heading not required.)

Army Form C. 2118

Place	Date	Hour	Summary of Events and Information	Remarks and references to Appendices
WESTR E- HEM.	6/2/16		Nothing unusual occurred today.	

A.E. Berry Major

WAR DIARY
or
INTELLIGENCE SUMMARY

(Erase heading not required.)

Army Form C. 2118

Place	Date	Hour	Summary of Events and Information	Remarks and references to Appendices
WESTRE-HEM.	7/2/16		Nothing unusual occurred today.	

A.E. Berry Major

WAR DIARY
or
INTELLIGENCE SUMMARY

Army Form C. 2118

Place	Date	Hour	Summary of Events and Information	Remarks and references to Appendices
WESTRE-HEM	8/2/16		Nothing unusual occurred today	

H.E. Berry Major

Army Form C. 2118

WAR DIARY
or
INTELLIGENCE SUMMARY
(Erase heading not required.)

Instructions regarding War Diaries and Intelligence Summaries are contained in F. S. Regs., Part II. and the Staff Manual respectively. Title Pages will be prepared in manuscript.

Place	Date	Hour	Summary of Events and Information	Remarks and references to Appendices
WESTRE-AEM.	9/2/16.		Nothing unusual occurred today.	

A. E. Berry Major

Army Form C. 2118

WAR DIARY
or
INTELLIGENCE SUMMARY
(Erase heading not required.)

Place	Date	Hour	Summary of Events and Information	Remarks and references to Appendices
WESTRE-HEM.	10/2/16		Nothing unusual occurred today.	

A. E. Berry Major

WAR DIARY
or
INTELLIGENCE SUMMARY

(Erase heading not required.)

Army Form C. 2118

Place	Date	Hour	Summary of Events and Information	Remarks and references to Appendices
WESTRE-HEM	11/2/16		Nothing unusual occurred today.	

A.E.Berry Major

WAR DIARY
or
INTELLIGENCE SUMMARY

(Erase heading not required.)

Army Form C. 2118

Instructions regarding War Diaries and Intelligence Summaries are contained in F. S. Regs., Part II. and the Staff Manual respectively. Title Pages will be prepared in manuscript.

Place	Date	Hour	Summary of Events and Information	Remarks and references to Appendices
WESTRE HEM.	12/9/16		Nothing unusual occurred today.	

H. E. Berry Major

WAR DIARY
or
INTELLIGENCE SUMMARY

Army Form C. 2118

Place	Date	Hour	Summary of Events and Information	Remarks and references to Appendices
WESTREHEM	13/2/16		Nothing unusual occurred today.	

H.E. Berry Major

Army Form C. 2118

WAR DIARY
or
INTELLIGENCE SUMMARY
(Erase heading not required.)

Place	Date	Hour	Summary of Events and Information	Remarks and references to Appendices
WESTRE-AEM	14/2/16		Nothing unusual occurred today	

A.E. Perry Major

WAR DIARY
or
INTELLIGENCE SUMMARY

Army Form C. 2118

Place	Date	Hour	Summary of Events and Information	Remarks and references to Appendices
WESTRE-HEM	15/2/16		Nothing unusual occurred today	

A.E.Berry Major

WAR DIARY
or
INTELLIGENCE SUMMARY

Army Form C. 2118

Place	Date	Hour	Summary of Events and Information	Remarks and references to Appendices
WESTRE-HEM.	16/2/16.		Nothing unusual occurred today.	

H.E. Berry Major

WAR DIARY
or
INTELLIGENCE SUMMARY

Army Form C. 2118

Place	Date	Hour	Summary of Events and Information	Remarks and references to Appendices
WESTRE-HEM.	17/2/16		Nothing unusual occurred today	

A E Berry Major

WAR DIARY
or
INTELLIGENCE SUMMARY

(Erase heading not required.)

Army Form C. 2118

Place	Date	Hour	Summary of Events and Information	Remarks and references to Appendices
WESTRE HEM.	18/9/16		Nothing unusual occurred today	

A.E. Berry Major

WAR DIARY or INTELLIGENCE SUMMARY

Place	Date	Hour	Summary of Events and Information	Remarks and references to Appendices
WESTRE-HEM	19/2/16		Nothing unusual occurred today	

H.E. Berry Major

WAR DIARY
INTELLIGENCE SUMMARY

Place	Date	Hour	Summary of Events and Information	Remarks and references to Appendices
WEMTRE-HEM.	20/9/16		Nothing unusual occurred today.	

H.E. Berry Major

Army Form C. 2118.

WAR DIARY
or
INTELLIGENCE SUMMARY

(Erase heading not required.)

Place	Date	Hour	Summary of Events and Information	Remarks and references to Appendices
WESTRE HEM	21/2/16		Nothing unusual occurred today.	

A.E. Berry / Major

Army Form C. 2118.

WAR DIARY
or
INTELLIGENCE SUMMARY

(Erase heading not required.)

Instructions regarding War Diaries and Intelligence Summaries are contained in F. S. Regs., Part II. and the Staff Manual respectively. Title Pages will be prepared in manuscript.

Place	Date	Hour	Summary of Events and Information	Remarks and references to Appendices
WESTRE-HEM	22/2/16		Nothing unusual occurred today	

H. E. Berry / Major

Army Form C. 2118.

WAR DIARY
or
INTELLIGENCE SUMMARY

(Erase heading not required.)

Place	Date	Hour	Summary of Events and Information	Remarks and references to Appendices
WESTRE-HEM	23/9/16		Nothing unusual occurred today.	

H.E. Berry Major

Army Form C. 2118.

WAR DIARY
or
INTELLIGENCE SUMMARY

(Erase heading not required.)

Instructions regarding War Diaries and Intelligence Summaries are contained in F. S. Regs., Part II. and the Staff Manual respectively. Title Pages will be prepared in manuscript.

Place	Date	Hour	Summary of Events and Information	Remarks and references to Appendices
WESTRE-HEM	24/9/16		Nothing unusual occurred today	

A. E. Berrey
Major

Army Form C. 2118.

WAR DIARY
or
INTELLIGENCE SUMMARY

(Erase heading not required.)

Instructions regarding War Diaries and Intelligence Summaries are contained in F. S. Regs., Part II. and the Staff Manual respectively. Title Pages will be prepared in manuscript.

Place	Date	Hour	Summary of Events and Information	Remarks and references to Appendices
WESTRE-HEM	25/9/16		Nothing unusual occurred today	

H. E. Berry Major

Army Form C. 2118.

WAR DIARY
or
INTELLIGENCE SUMMARY

(Erase heading not required.)

Place	Date	Hour	Summary of Events and Information	Remarks and references to Appendices
WESTRE-HEM	9/7/16		Nothing unusual occurred today.	

A.E. Berry Major

WAR DIARY
INTELLIGENCE SUMMARY

Place	Date	Hour	Summary of Events and Information	Remarks and references to Appendices
MESIRE-AEM	27/5/16		Nothing unusual occurred today	

A.E. Berry, Major

WAR DIARY
INTELLIGENCE SUMMARY

Army Form C. 2118.

Place	Date	Hour	Summary of Events and Information	Remarks and references to Appendices
CANTRAIWE	28/9/16		Moved from WESTREHEM to CANTRAIWE today a distance of 7 miles. Roads very slippery after frosty night. No casualties en route.	

A.E. Berry. Major

WAR DIARY
or
INTELLIGENCE SUMMARY

Army Form C. 2118.

Place	Date	Hour	Summary of Events and Information	Remarks and references to Appendices
CANTRAIMVE	29/9/16		Nothing unusual occurred today.	

A.E Berry Major

Confidential

C. Sqdn. South Irish Horse.

War Diary - March 1916

Army Form C. 2118.

WAR DIARY
or
INTELLIGENCE SUMMARY

(*Erase heading not required.*)

Place	Date	Hour	Summary of Events and Information	Remarks and references to Appendices
CANTRAIMVE	1/3/16		Nothing unusual occurred today. E.K.J.	

H.E. Berrythayn

Army Form C. 2118.

WAR DIARY
or
INTELLIGENCE SUMMARY
(Erase heading not required.)

Instructions regarding War Diaries and Intelligence Summaries are contained in F. S. Regs., Part II. and the Staff Manual respectively. Title Pages will be prepared in manuscript.

Place	Date	Hour	Summary of Events and Information	Remarks and references to Appendices
CANTRAINNE	2/3/16		Nothing unusual occurred today.	

Major

Army Form C. 2118.

WAR DIARY
INTELLIGENCE SUMMARY

Place	Date	Hour	Summary of Events and Information	Remarks and references to Appendices
CANTRAIMNE	3/3/16		Nothing unusual occurred today. [JS]	

H.E. Berry Major

WAR DIARY
INTELLIGENCE SUMMARY

Army Form C. 2118.

Place	Date	Hour	Summary of Events and Information	Remarks and references to Appendices
CAMBRAINNE	4/3/16		A party of 3 Officers & 12 N.C.O.s proceeded to reconnoitre & report on state of roads leading from an assembly area found LABOURSE in the direction of the trenches beyond VERMELLES. Snowing nearly all day, consequently horses were unable to travel the roads without. Completing the but to return home without. Completing the recon once more.	

J.F.

H.E. Berry Major

Army Form C. 2118.

WAR DIARY
or
INTELLIGENCE SUMMARY

(Erase heading not required.)

Instructions regarding War Diaries and Intelligence Summaries are contained in F. S. Regs., Part II. and the Staff Manual respectively. Title Pages will be prepared in manuscript.

Place	Date	Hour	Summary of Events and Information	Remarks and references to Appendices
CANTRAINE	5/3/16		Same party proceeded to area indly. for completed reconnaissance. During day.	

Major

Army Form C. 2118.

WAR DIARY
or
INTELLIGENCE SUMMARY

(Erase heading not required.)

Place	Date	Hour	Summary of Events and Information	Remarks and references to Appendices
CAMRAI NNE	6/3/16		Nothing unusual occurred today.	

A E Berry Major

Army Form C. 2118.

WAR DIARY
or
INTELLIGENCE SUMMARY

(Erase heading not required.)

Place	Date	Hour	Summary of Events and Information	Remarks and references to Appendices
CANTRAIMNE	7/3/16		Nothing unusual occurred today	

A.E. Berry Major

Army Form C. 2118.

WAR DIARY
or
INTELLIGENCE SUMMARY
(Erase heading not required.)

Place	Date	Hour	Summary of Events and Information	Remarks and references to Appendices
CAMTRAINVE	6/3/16		Nothing much of occurred to day.	

Major

Army Form C. 2118.

WAR DIARY
or
INTELLIGENCE SUMMARY

(Erase heading not required.)

Place	Date	Hour	Summary of Events and Information	Remarks and references to Appendices
HURION-VILLE	9/3/16		The Squadron moved from CANTRAISSAI to their new billets at HURIONVILLE a distance of 3 miles. Fine cold day.	

Army Form C. 2118.

WAR DIARY
or
INTELLIGENCE SUMMARY

(Erase heading not required.)

Place	Date	Hour	Summary of Events and Information	Remarks and references to Appendices
HURIDN-VIELE	10/3/16		Nothing unusual occurred today. Very cold weather.	

H.E. Berryman Major.

WAR DIARY
or
INTELLIGENCE SUMMARY

Army Form C. 2118.

Place	Date	Hour	Summary of Events and Information	Remarks and references to Appendices
CHURION-VILLE	11/3/16		Fifty men from the Squadron were employed on Police Duty in connection with a scheme being carried out by 25th Division. Cold dry weather. J.B.	

L.E. Danny
Major.

Army Form C. 2118.

WAR DIARY
or
INTELLIGENCE SUMMARY

(Erase heading not required.)

Instructions regarding War Diaries and Intelligence Summaries are contained in F. S. Regs., Part II. and the Staff Manual respectively. Title Pages will be prepared in manuscript.

Place	Date	Hour	Summary of Events and Information	Remarks and references to Appendices
HURION-VILLE	19/3/16		Same scheme of Police Duty carried out by 2 squadron. One man dog.	

A.S.

of E Berry Major.

Army Form C. 2118.

WAR DIARY
or
INTELLIGENCE SUMMARY

(Erase heading not required.)

Place	Date	Hour	Summary of Events and Information	Remarks and references to Appendices
HURION-VILLE	13/3/16		Nothing unusual occurred today. Fine day.	

D.N.

H.E. Berry Major.

Army Form C. 2118.

WAR DIARY
or
INTELLIGENCE SUMMARY

(Erase heading not required.)

Place	Date	Hour	Summary of Events and Information	Remarks and references to Appendices
HURION-VILLE	14/3/16		Nothing unusual occurred today. Fine warm day.	

LNJ.

F.O Dinny Major

Army Form C. 2118.

WAR DIARY
or
INTELLIGENCE SUMMARY

(Erase heading not required.)

Place	Date	Hour	Summary of Events and Information	Remarks and references to Appendices
HURION-VILLE	15/3/16		Nothing unusual occurred today. Warm day. Fatigue party of 1 NCO and 10 men proceeded to repair road between this place and BURBURE. Material was bought by our own labour from slag heaps at RAIMBERT.	

F.E. Berry Major.

WAR DIARY
or
INTELLIGENCE SUMMARY

(Erase heading not required.)

Army Form C. 2118.

Place	Date	Hour	Summary of Events and Information	Remarks and references to Appendices
HURION-VILLE	16/3/16		1 N.C.O. & 10 men proceeded to Corps Hd Qrs as escort to Gen Gough. Fine warm day.	

PMJ

A. E. Berry Major

Army Form C. 2118.

WAR DIARY
or
INTELLIGENCE SUMMARY

(Erase heading not required.)

Instructions regarding War Diaries and Intelligence Summaries are contained in F. S. Regs., Part II. and the Staff Manual respectively. Title Pages will be prepared in manuscript.

Place	Date	Hour	Summary of Events and Information	Remarks and references to Appendices
HURION-VILLE	17/3/16		St. Patrick's Day. Nothing unusual occurred today. Fine warm day.	
do	18/3/16		Nothing unusual occurred today. Fine warm day.	
do	19/3/16		Nothing unusual occurred today. Fine warm day.	

EAB

Lt E Bailey Major

Army Form C. 2118.

WAR DIARY
or
INTELLIGENCE SUMMARY

(Erase heading not required.)

Instructions regarding War Diaries and Intelligence Summaries are contained in F. S. Regs., Part II. and the Staff Manual respectively. Title Pages will be prepared in manuscript.

Place	Date	Hour	Summary of Events and Information	Remarks and references to Appendices
HURION-VILLE	20/3/16		Nothing unusual occurred today. D.G.	

& E Berry
Major

Army Form C. 2118.

WAR DIARY
or
INTELLIGENCE SUMMARY

(Erase heading not required.)

Place	Date	Hour	Summary of Events and Information	Remarks and references to Appendices
HURION-VILLE	21/3/16		Nothing unusual occurred today. Rainy day	
	22/3/16		Nothing unusual occurred today. Raining day.	
	23/3/16		Do. Fine day	
	24/3/16		Do. Fine day but cold	
	25/3/16		Do. Rainy cold day.	

H. E. Berry Major

WAR DIARY
or
INTELLIGENCE SUMMARY

Army Form C. 2118.

Place	Date	Hour	Summary of Events and Information	Remarks and references to Appendices
HURION- VILLE	26/3/16		Nothing unusual occurred today.	
	27/3/16		The Squadron moved from HURIONVILLE to VAUDRICOURT. The Division holds now a portion of the line.	
VAUDRI- COURT	28/3/16		Nothing unusual occurred today.	
	29/3/16		1 Officer & 30 men proceeded to LOOS to be attached to the 47th Bde Signal Company for duty in connexion with laying of cables	

Major
ot 2 Diary

WAR DIARY
or
INTELLIGENCE SUMMARY

Army Form C. 2118.

Place	Date	Hour	Summary of Events and Information	Remarks and references to Appendices
VAUDRI-COURT.	30/3/16		Nothing unusual occurred today. Fine day.	
	31/3/16		Do. Fine warm day.	

H E Berry Major

Confidential

War Diary XVI

"C" Squadron — South Irish Horse

Month of April 1916.

Army Form C. 2118.

WAR DIARY
or
INTELLIGENCE SUMMARY
(Erase heading not required.)

Place	Date	Hour	Summary of Events and Information	Remarks and references to Appendices
VAUDRI-COURT.	1/4/16		Nothing unusual occurred today. Fine warm day.	
	2/4/16		Nothing unusual occurred today. Fine warm weather.	
	3/4/16		Nothing unusual occurred today. Warm weather	
	4/4/16		Do	
	5/4/16		Do	

H.E. Berry Major

Army Form C. 2118.

WAR DIARY
or
INTELLIGENCE SUMMARY

(Erase heading not required.)

Place	Date	Hour	Summary of Events and Information	Remarks and references to Appendices
VAUDRI-COURT	6/4/16		3 men proceeded to LILLERS to be attached to Town Major for duty. Fine day.	
	7/4/16		Nothing unusual occurred today. Fine cold day.	
	8/4/16		Advance guard scheme with cyclists on high ground in neighbourhood of LABEUVRIERE. Fine day.	
	9/4/16		Nothing unusual occurred today. Fine day. Working parts returned from trenches.	

J.E. Berry Major

Army Form C. 2118.

WAR DIARY
or
INTELLIGENCE SUMMARY

(*Erase heading not required.*)

Instructions regarding War Diaries and Intelligence Summaries are contained in F. S. Regs., Part II. and the Staff Manual respectively. Title Pages will be prepared in manuscript.

Place	Date	Hour	Summary of Events and Information	Remarks and references to Appendices
VAUDRI- COURT.	10/4/16		Nothing unusual occurred today	
	11/4/16		do	
	12/4/16		do	
	13/4/16		do Draft of 8 men arrived.	
	14/4/16		do	
	15/4/16		Scheme with Cy drill in neighbourhood of RUITZ	
	16/4/16		Nothing unusual occurred today.	

A.E. Berry Major

Army Form C. 2118.

WAR DIARY
or
INTELLIGENCE SUMMARY

(Erase heading not required.)

Place	Date	Hour	Summary of Events and Information	Remarks and references to Appendices
VAUDRI- COURT	17/4/16		Nothing unusual occurred today	
	18/4/16		do	
	19/4/16		do	
	20/4/16		do	
	21/4/16		do.	
	22/4/16		Scheme with cyclists in neighbourhood of TOUQUEREIL.	
	23/4/16		Nothing unusual occurred today	

D.S.
Major

Army Form C. 2118.

WAR DIARY
or
INTELLIGENCE SUMMARY

(Erase heading not required.)

Instructions regarding War Diaries and Intelligence Summaries are contained in F. S. Regs., Part II. and the Staff Manual respectively. Title Pages will be prepared in manuscript.

Place	Date	Hour	Summary of Events and Information	Remarks and references to Appendices
MAUDRI-COURT	24/4/16		Nothing unusual occurred today	
	25/4/16		do	
	26/4/16		do	
	27/4/16		do	
	28/4/16		do	
	29/4/16		do	
	30/4/16		do	

H E Burke Major

Army Form C. 2118.

WAR DIARY
or
INTELLIGENCE SUMMARY
(Erase heading not required.)

Instructions regarding War Diaries and Intelligence Summaries are contained in F. S. Regs., Part II. and the Staff Manual respectively. Title Pages will be prepared in manuscript.

Place	Date	Hour	Summary of Events and Information	Remarks and references to Appendices
VAUDRI-COURT	1/5/16		Nothing unusual occurred today	
	2/5/16		do	do	
	3/5/16		do	do	
	4/5/16		do	do	
	5/5/16		do	do	
	6/5/16		do	do	
	7/5/16		do	do	

DJS

A. True Copy
For Major

Army Form C. 2118.

WAR DIARY
or
INTELLIGENCE SUMMARY

(Erase heading not required.)

Instructions regarding War Diaries and Intelligence Summaries are contained in F. S. Regs., Part II. and the Staff Manual respectively. Title Pages will be prepared in manuscript.

Place	Date	Hour	Summary of Events and Information	Remarks and references to Appendices
VAUDRI-COURT.	8/5/16		Nothing unusual occurred today	
	9/5/16		do	
	10/5/16		do	
	11/5/16		Party of 25 men for work in connection with stragglers posts called for at 7.50 p.m. This party returned at 1.30 a.m. on conclusion of attack	
	12/5/16		Nothing unusual occurred today	
	13/5/16		do	

D.J.S.

J. Grant Capt
for J. Hagan

Army Form C. 2118.

WAR DIARY
or
INTELLIGENCE SUMMARY

(Erase heading not required.)

Instructions regarding War Diaries and Intelligence Summaries are contained in F. S. Regs., Part II. and the Staff Manual respectively. Title Pages will be prepared in manuscript.

Place	Date	Hour	Summary of Events and Information	Remarks and references to Appendices
VAUDRI-COURT	14/5/16		Nothing unusual occurred today	
	15/5/16		1 Officer & 30 men proceeded to VERMELLES as a working party in connexion with trench maintenance	
	16/5/16		Nothing unusual occurred today	
	17/5/16		The Squadron from this date forming up with S. & E Squadrons was formed into Corps troops.	
	18/5/16		Nothing unusual occurred today	
	19/5/16		do	
	20/5/16		do	

D.M.

E.J.Grant
Capt.

Army Form C. 2118.

WAR DIARY
or
INTELLIGENCE SUMMARY

(Erase heading not required.)

Place	Date	Hour	Summary of Events and Information	Remarks and references to Appendices
MAUDRI- COURT	21/5/16		Nothing unusual occurred today	
	22/5/16		do do	
	23/5/16		do do	
	24/5/16		do do	
	25/5/16		do do	
	26/5/16		do do	
	27/5/16		do do	
			E.J.	
			E.J. Grant Capt.	

Army Form C. 2118.

WAR DIARY
or
INTELLIGENCE SUMMARY

(Erase heading not required.)

Instructions regarding War Diaries and Intelligence Summaries are contained in F. S. Regs., Part II and the Staff Manual respectively. Title Pages will be prepared in manuscript.

Place	Date	Hour	Summary of Events and Information	Remarks and references to Appendices
VAUDRI-COURT	28/5/16		Nothing unusual occurred today	
	29/5/16		Trench party returned, also 10 men who had been acting as escort to 1st Corps Commander.	
	30/5/16		Squadron left VAUDRICOURT at 8 a.m. in full marching order en route for 1st Division training area arriving at COYECQUE at 6 p.m. where it billeted for the night.	
	31/5/16		Left COYECQUE at 9 a.m. & arrived HESDIGNEUL 6.30 p.m. Horses were picketed out on arrival men billeted in a big farm. Horses were shod the journey of 50 miles well.	

A.J. Nevil.
Capt.

www.ingramcontent.com/pod-product-compliance
Lightning Source LLC
Chambersburg PA
CBHW081433160426
43193CB00013B/2265